Cartoons for Joseph Selleny

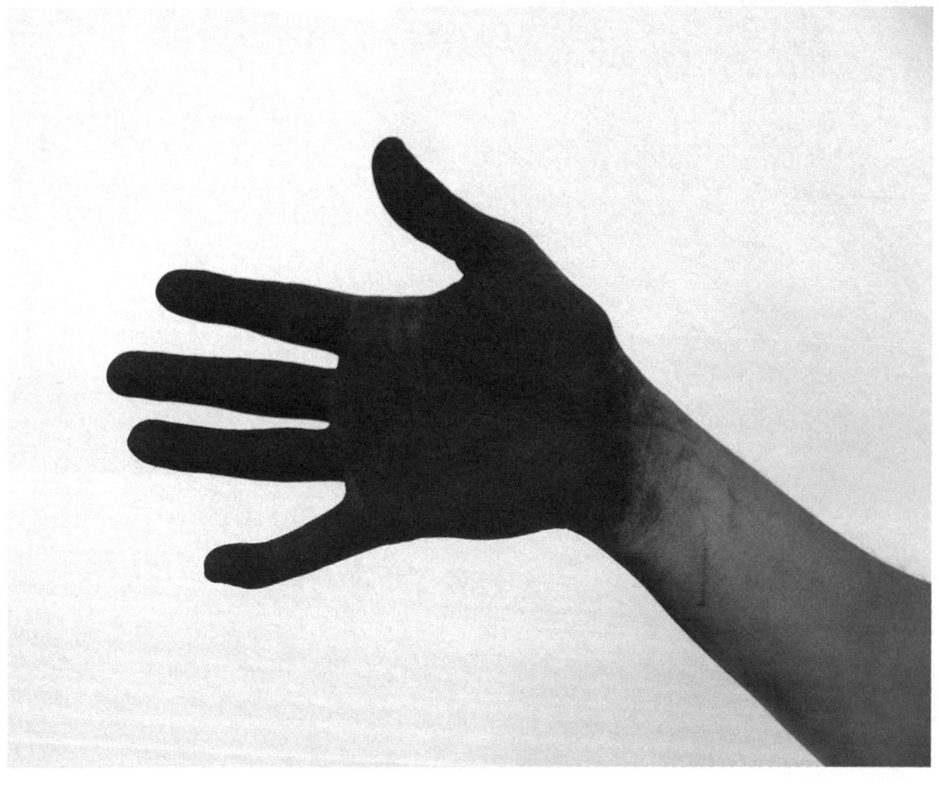

Dear

Good to see you in the studio yesterday, and thanks for your help with the trial wall drawing. I liked what you said about the wall drawing and the cartoons when we paused for lunch. I'm always conscious of charcoal as particles. That's part of how it makes such matte blacks, but also an important difference to painting, which makes a slick, a kind of continuous sheet on the surface of the image. Our conversation yesterday seemed to gravitate around this: charcoal works by disaggregating as you draw. Certainly the pouncing we were doing yesterday — beating those perforated drawings with ground-up charcoal wrapped in cheesecloth — relies on this characteristic of the medium. There's something fascinating about the way those little specks of burnt wood become airborne and make their way through the perforations in the cartoons, reconstituting themselves as a landscape of dots on the wall behind, the surface beneath the images we were also beginning to unmake with that pouncing.

Enclosed is a print of one of the photos you took with my camera when we stopped for lunch (which attests to how much charcoal was made airborne during that morning).

I also meant to give you the Badiou book we discussed last week as we sat drinking at the edge of the Harbour in Sydney, listening to the water moving around us as we talked. It is enclosed here. It's a surprisingly fast read. The passages about love and theatre towards the end are the parts I thought you might find interesting, though I find the whole text wonderful and it made me think a lot about how love figures in the desires we hold and gestate in art-making.

See you next week.
Tom

Dear [redacted]

It's the very end of a long day, the first full day of work since I arrived in Vienna, and the first day in the underground store at the Museum für Völkerkunde, the Vienna Ethnographic Museum. I was two storeys under the ground all day, looking at the objects brought back on the *Novara* after her circumnavigation of the globe, those objects from Sydney and the Illawarra taken during the six weeks the frigate spent on the waters of Sydney Harbour. (By the way, I forgot to mention when we met that the *Novara* always carried a gondola with it, and during the stay in Sydney the crew made gondola trips around Sydney Harbour. What a strange echo of those Eora fishing boats it must have been.) It rained all day, unbelievably heavily, and even down there, deep underground, I could hear the water the whole time, in a way that reminded me of the torrential rain during the drive back to Sydney from Wreck Bay after Jonathan and I visited you.

Tomorrow I'll go back and look at more of the *Novara* objects, and begin to go through the Museum filing systems, to glean what information I can.

Once I've collated all the information I've managed to pull together I'll write a proper letter, with a full set of photos, but, in the interim, I just wanted to let you know that I looked at 18 objects from the *Novara* today. I was constantly reminded of being with you all only a week or

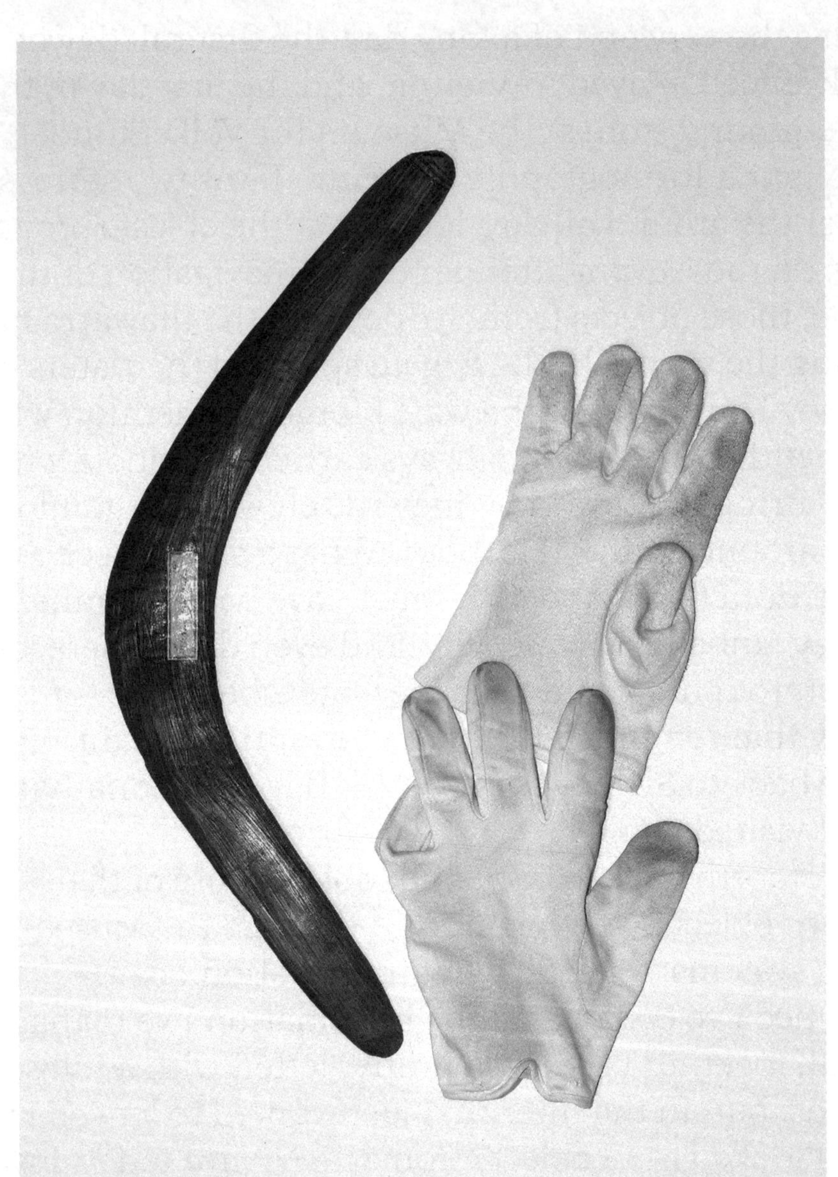

so ago, and of specific words, stories, and ways of handling objects which you put to me.

Enclosed is a photo of one of the three boomerangs I looked at (they're all labelled as being from New South Wales). The gloves hopefully give you some sense of scale (as well as a sense of the amount of dust those gloves accumulated handling those objects). The boomerang balanced on my finger, just the way you showed me. It also had a very smoothed-out little area where I guess a hand — or many hands — had held it over a long time. Like many of the objects I looked at and handled, I was conscious that this boomerang was already very old when it was taken in 1858. I wrapped my hand inside the handle of one of the parrying shields — it was pretty rough all over its visible surface — and suddenly felt a part of the object's surface I could not see: an intense smoothness that felt like the accumulation of many, many hands upon that object. It was very moving to feel that age, that sense of that object being carried, used, slowly worn down by all those hours and hours and hours, an accumulation of time that was also kept from my seeing, only discernible through my hands. I wondered if many of these objects dated back to well before the invasion. I also felt conscious that it should be your hands that handle these things, and that no amount of photographs and words written to you can make up for you not being able to hold each object, grasp its weight, and try to imagine its life through how it feels.

You said a great thing about the wind, about there

being many words to describe different kinds of wind. I was reminded of that yesterday. At the very end of the day I paid a visit to the truly amazing Naturhistorisches Museum, the Natural History Museum (not far from the Ethnographic Museum), which has something like 7 or 8 huge halls filled with cases of stuffed birds, the biggest collection on earth apparently. There are a lot of Australian birds in there, lyrebirds, sulphur-crested cockatoos, emus, galahs, etc. Being there was less an experience of empiricism or science and more like a very extended apparition. It was deeply strange to see all those feathers, in room after room, case after case, but with no wind to ruffle them. Museums — and especially museum cases — are seemingly wind-less spaces, and it was the same today with those objects in the underground storeroom of the Ethnographic Museum. There's no wind down there, no movement of air around those objects. But holding some of these objects, I could imagine them animated again. The hours and hours and hours of these things being handled, touched, and used wears them down, but in a funny way also gives them weight. I began to imagine the life and living of which those objects were a part — and this in turn gave life to those objects, even in that wind-less storeroom ten feet under the ground.

One disappointing bit of news: as I said, I looked at 18 objects today, and there are 6 spears for me to look at tomorrow. But the other 50 or so things that were taken by the *Novara* from Sydney in 1858, and that are in the

Museum catalogue and the *Novara*'s inventory, seem to be lost. In the 1920s the Ethnography Department of the Natural History Museum split off to become its own museum, the Museum für Völkerkunde. The curator I have been dealing with was very mystified when I told her about these objects being missing. After consulting with her colleagues and the catalogue records, she concluded that the moment the Museum split off from the Natural History Museum is the point at which those objects can no longer be traced. So, somewhere in some odd corner of the Natural History Museum, there are 50 or so objects that were meant to go to the new Ethnography Museum but never made it. I'm hoping there might be a way to find those objects and have emailed one of the Museum's curators.

I hope you are all going well.

Warmest regards,
Tom

P.S. Tomorrow I visit the Albertina to see the drawings made by the artist who travelled on the *Novara*, Joseph Selleny, who made some interesting portraits of Aboriginal men and women from the Illawarra during a trip he made down to Wollongong from Sydney. The Albertina's collection includes a drawing he made sitting above Sydney Harbour, overlooking that spectacular body of water that was in my mind for most of today.

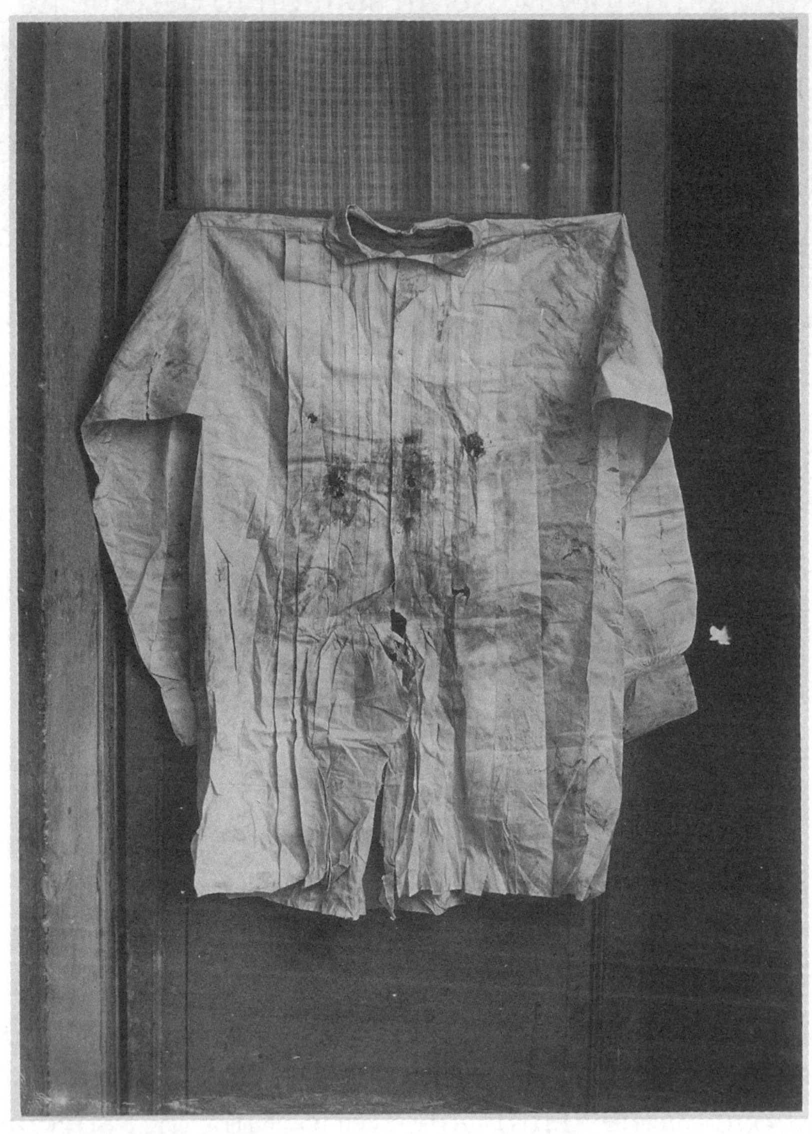

Dear [redacted]

Today I visited Maximilian's tomb. (A Mexican visitor before me had left a letter at his tomb, a letter dated today but addressed to someone who died 140 years ago.) I am sure you have also visited this place, the *Kaisergruft*, two storeys under the ground in central Vienna, full of all those strange ornate tombs encasing the remains of Hapsburg royalty. Were you there when the *Novara* brought back Maximilian's bullet-riddled body from Mexico?

I spent last week looking at your drawings from your time on the *Novara*, including a very beautiful drawing of Sydney Harbour, drawn from Darling Point, looking towards Sydney Cove. Its vividness made me imagine you sitting there, overlooking that great expanse of water. It's a drawing you would have made quickly, not much longer than a snapshot, but long enough to make you feel the elements, the way making a drawing outdoors makes you feel the wind and weather upon your body. That sense of the wind upon your skin was even stronger for me in your drawings of the open ocean, made on the deck of the *Novara*. I find them stunning, as drawings dedicated to how wind makes itself visible upon a surface (the surface of the ocean), an intricate and indeterminate set of effects in turn visited upon another surface (the surface of the paper). It made me wonder about how you made them, sitting out on deck, the surface of your body subject to the same piercing wind. It reminded me of a windy night when I was at art school, taking a charcoal drawing outside to spray it with fixative, and bringing it back into the studio to see that the image had disappeared without trace, the charcoal having been blown off the surface of the paper in the pitch black darkness outside.

I am working on drawings of Manet's four paintings *The Execution of Maximilian*, a set of cartoons for that series of paintings, preparatory drawings after the fact. Have you seen these paintings? I assume you've seen the photographs taken after the event (like this image of Maximilian's shirt, which I have enclosed), but what do you make of Manet's painting, the coolness of the way it captures that moment when the resistance to the invasion ends in execution, those bullet holes? Did you ever think about making an image from that moment, a painting of that event, the execution of your patron, someone you spent all those hours and hours alongside on the *Novara*?

Yours sincerely,
Tom Nicholson

Dear 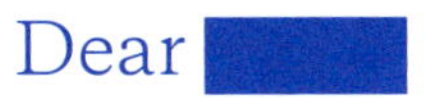

Thank you for meeting up earlier this week. It was great to meet you after spending all that time last week with your great uncle's drawings in the Albertina.

Selleny was a remarkable draughtsman — I'd already sensed this from the drawings I'd seen in Wollongong, two really beautiful drawings from Mount Keira (including the Osborne Wallsend coalmine, one of the first places in Australia where they began to dig coal out of the ground, something Australians have not stopped doing ever since!). Incidentally, by chance that day in the storeroom at the Wollongong City Gallery, I saw another work by a very wonderful woman, the Gorawarl/ Jerrawongarla elder and artist, Aunty Julie Freeman, an image of the same mountain where Selleny sat and looked through the thick forest towards the water to make those two drawings. If you ever make it out to Australia, I hope you get to see her works alongside those of your great uncle.

The Albertina drawings from Selleny's time on the *Novara* are really beautiful. The drawing he made *en plein air* high up on Darling Point, overlooking Sydney Harbour, is incredibly evocative of that sublime expanse of water. It has been in my mind ever since I saw it.

And thank you for bringing along his original *Tagebuch* from the *Novara* when we met up. What an extraordinary object it is: the slow encroachment of coal

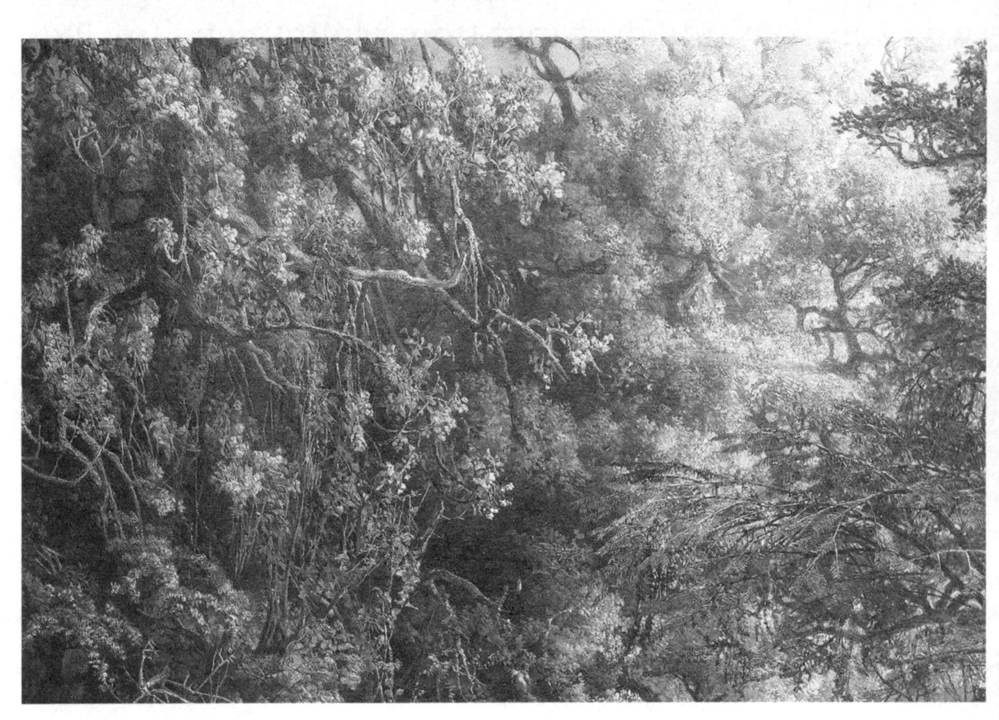

dust gradually swallowing up his meticulous writing as you move through it. I was very sorry that his diary entries from the six weeks the *Novara* spent on Sydney Harbour are in the part of the *Tagebuch* that is now completely obliterated by that black dust. (Though I also feel grateful to that coal cellar for preserving the diary underground for all those years, keeping it safe from the war, the bombs, the fires.)

I imagine you have good reproductions of this painting, but I have enclosed a detail from Selleny's last painting, *Australischer Urwald*, a photograph that I snapped when I saw it yesterday in the underground store of the Wien Museum. I could not find a way to photograph the painting in its totality in a way that adequately captured the extraordinary excess of its detail, a baroqueness that is both empirically true to the wonderful abundance of the rainforests in that part of New South Wales but that also gives the painting the suggestion of a hallucination. (Given that he made the painting a decade after he had been there, perhaps it is more a hallucination than an act of recording.) The date of the painting is interesting — 1867. He made that last painting the same year Maximilian was executed in Mexico.

I look forward to visiting you next week and seeing those Selleny paintings you have at home.

Warmest regards, and thanks,
Tom

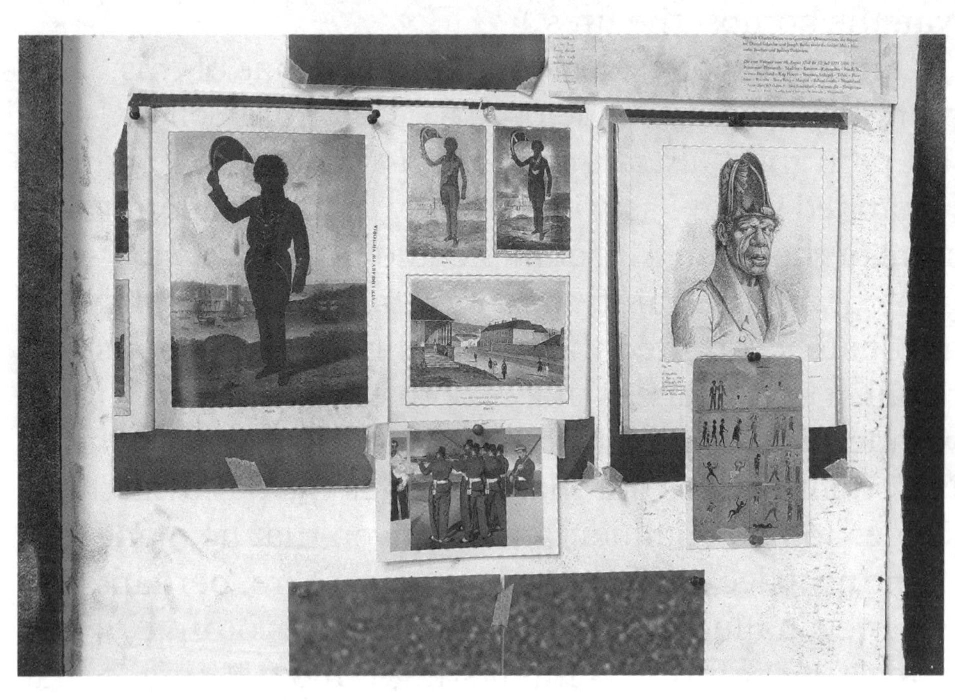

Dear ██████

It was great to meet up when you were passing through, and to show you the studio, and the drawings in progress.

You asked if I could send you a photograph of that part of my studio wall we were talking about (a photo is enclosed: a detail of that mass of source material, including all those images of Bungaree, with the marks of charcoal hands all over them, continuing the blackening out that the bad photocopy began!).

We were somehow distracted from the conversation about Bungaree. I started to pin up all those versions of his image on the studio wall in part because they seem to weirdly join up to the Manet *Execution* image, to slot into its missing parts. But it was actually Keith Vincent Smith who first led me to Bungaree. As you probably know, Keith has a hunch that Scherzer took his skull back to Vienna on the *Novara*, as an anthropological specimen, having traded for it with the Museum in Sydney (which is reported to have received it as a donation on 9 December 1857, but now has no record of it). It would certainly fit with Scherzer's behaviour during the *Novara*'s stay in Sydney. (One of the most powerful things on your *Novara* website is the way you present Scherzer's unofficial *Tagebuch*, with all those really disturbing descriptions of them digging up Aboriginal remains, alongside the famous, published, sanitised account, where all that is edited out, papered over.)

There is nothing in the records of the Natural History Museum in Vienna to support Keith's hunch, but when I met with the curator of the Anthropology Department at the Museum, she said a lot of that material ended up in the collection of the Medical University.

I have been thinking about Bungaree quite a bit lately. Before I left to come here I was down at Indented Head, near Melbourne, one of the places where Bungaree came ashore (in April 1802) as part of Flinders' party when they were circumnavigating Australia. There's a monument there (though it only mentions Flinders, not Bungaree). I always feel slightly ambivalent about the title often given to Bungaree: the first Aboriginal person to circumnavigate Australia. Rather than the celebrated line Flinders was able to produce through that circumnavigation — that very beautiful and impressively accurate outline of the shape of the continent — I find myself thinking about *points*, like Indented Head, where they came ashore, where Bungaree led negotiations with local Aboriginal people. It's a pity there's not a map of points — an archipelago of dots marking out these hundreds and hundreds of places where complex and ambiguous negotiations unfolded — as famous as that continuous line of Flinders' map.

I have now managed to fix an appointment with one of the researchers at the Anatomy Department at the Medical University. I will let you know how I go.

And I look forward to seeing you when I'm in Wollongong early next year.

Warm regards,
Tom

P.S. I also meant to talk with you about that early history of the *Novara*, its construction in the Arsenale in Venice during Austrian rule there. I find it extraordinary that the revolution of 1848 begins in the boatbuilding yards, with Manin seizing and re-naming the ship *Italia*, but also that the eventual name of the boat, the *Novara*, commemorates the final defeat of Manin and the anti-Austrian revolutionaries in the city of Novara. Even before it circumnavigates the globe, before it comes to Sydney, before it takes Maximilian to Mexico to take up his position as the puppet colonial Emperor (not to mention bringing back his corpse), the ship is inscribed with a struggle against colonial subjugation, and its vanquishing. It's a prehistory that gives a different edge to the image of the gondola on Sydney Harbour.

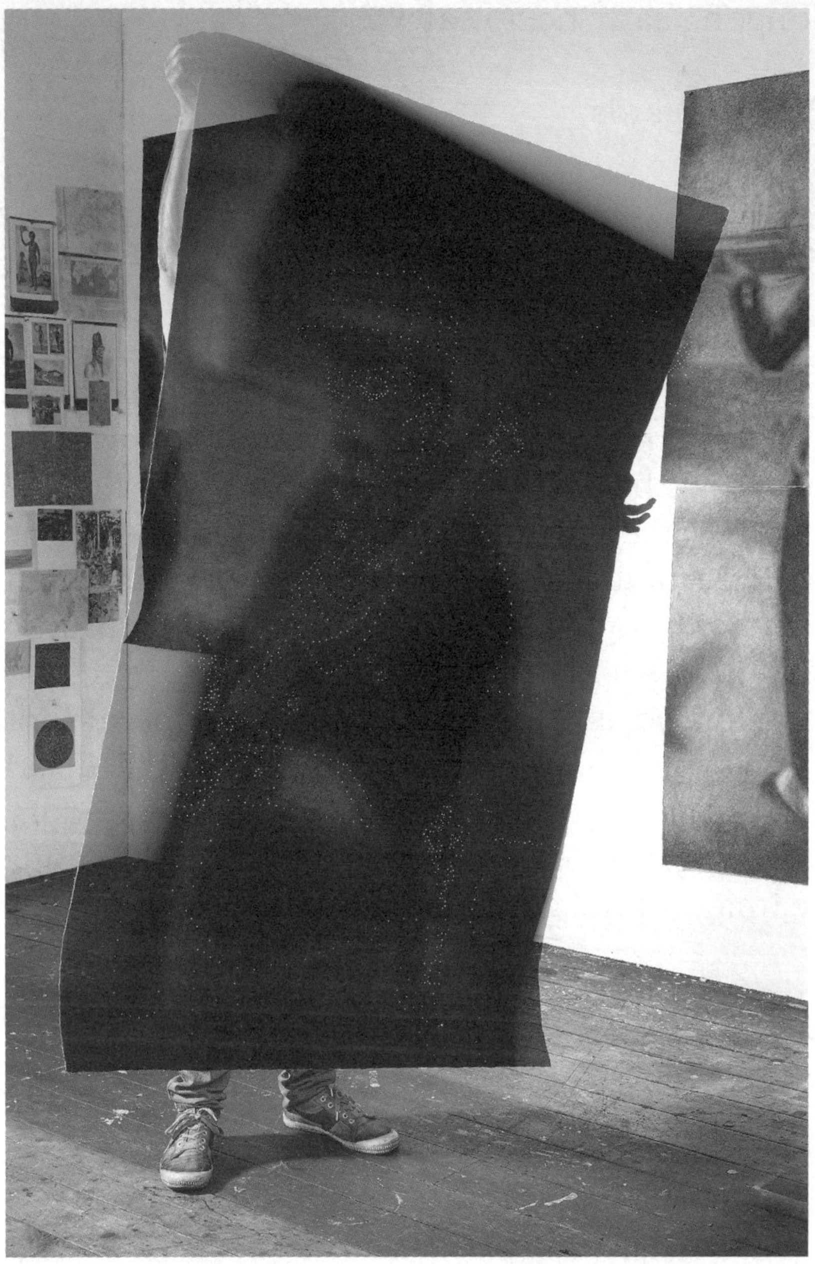

Hi [redacted]

Good to talk on the phone last night.

Enclosed is your copy of Clendinnen's *Dancing with Strangers*. It was an amazing experience to read it while I was staying in Sydney, staying right on the Harbour, walking each day along the edge of the water, returning home each evening to watch the blue out my window, reading Clendinnen, thinking about that moment at the very beginning of the British arrival, the space from which the whole invasion eventually unfolds. I have just started Karsken's book, and I do like the way at the beginning she gently criticises Clendinnen, that in that extraordinary early image of British soldiers dancing with Aboriginal men on the shores of Sydney Harbour, just a few days after they arrive, there is a precondition for that brief moment of conviviality, a precondition that must not be forgotten: the soldiers watching, guns at the ready. I feel like the Harbour always bears that spectre of violence, the brute reality of what begins here.

It was great to head down to Wreck Bay again yesterday, meet with Aunty Julie and have a long cup of tea with her. She talked a lot about Wreck Bay itself, the way it was a space where people fleeing violence and control elsewhere in New South Wales could come and cultivate a kind of autonomy. She also talked about the ships heading to Sydney that were regularly wrecked there, how the community would go out to rescue people, but would also end up with a lot of the objects from those ships. The dining table we were sitting at, drinking tea and talking around, was apparently from one of those ships. She talked about how those objects, tools, clothes, etc., helped them survive there, relatively independently, at that exposed place lashed by the wind, too windy for the British. I used that word you used to me—'visitation'—about how those objects appeared there. And you're right, there's something similar about my appearances at her doorstep, the arrival of someone or something from elsewhere, perhaps in some ways not so dissimilar from Selleny appearing suddenly in the Illawarra in 1858 to make drawings of the landscape and its people during the *Novara*'s stay on Sydney Harbour. To me the objects in her house from all those ships were a beautiful inversion of the *Novara* and its classically 19th-century European mandate to collect—collecting as a parallel activity to circumnavigating, two ways to try to establish and show knowing, both activities finding their means in the object of the ship. Aunty Julie talks a lot about staying on her patch, and in the case of that patch, Wreck Bay, and all those shipwrecks, the wind makes the ships give up their objects to the world, not the other way around.

I talked with her about being in Vienna, seeing those objects in the underground store at the Museum of Ethnography, and particularly about feeling the smoothness inside that shield against my hand (the one I was talking about last night). We talked about the meaning of that accumulation — those years and years of hands — for those objects, and their weight.

We talked a lot about Sydney Harbour too. When she goes there, she said, she often has in her mind the image of Jervis Bay, the grasses and trees and bushes running to the water's edge, and she imagines what the Harbour must have looked like before 1788. She described an extremely beautiful image to me: the Harbour at night, populated by Eora boats, each with a small fire upon a clay pan, both a way to attract fish with the fire's light, and a means to immediately cook them once they're caught. The Harbour, she said, becomes a night sky, a dark expanse dotted with pinpricks of light, an image that dwelt powerfully in my head as I flew back to Melbourne last night, imagining looking down upon that expanse of starry night sky from the aeroplane above.

I have also enclosed a photo, taken while I was working on the trial wall drawing in the studio, moving one of the cartoons into place to 'pounce' it (i.e., beat the cartoon, the perforated drawing, with charcoal dust to make the abstracted drawing on to the wall behind). Till now, I have tended to think of the wall drawing as a view of the night sky inverted, with each star a little charcoaly mass of dark light. But now I wonder if it becomes the negative of Aunty Julie's image of the Harbour, the aggregation of thousands of those fires, like the smoothness of that shield, a kind of register of accumulation, an accumulation of fires burnt on the waters of Sydney Harbour.

See you next week for the meeting at Coranderrk.

Cheers,
Tom

P.S. Do you remember that conversation we had about Barak last week, about the extraordinary arc of violence and dispossession around Melbourne that he witnessed in his lifetime? It occurred to me last night that the same could be said of Bungaree, who was a boy in 1788, and died in 1830. He witnessed those first four decades. He witnessed the process that unfolded from the space he inhabited, from Sydney Harbour. It must have been all the more acute for Bungaree, given how much of the continent he saw during the circumnavigation with Flinders. It's hard to fathom the accumulative effect of all the encounters during that voyage, encounters with other peoples at different moments of dispossession, subject to different kinds of violence, as well as with those for whom (he must have known) the dispossessing, the violence, lay in the future, a kind of witnessing before the fact.

Dear ████

It's been hectic since I left. On the way back I had two very good days in London, one of which was dedicated to the National Gallery. The main purpose of my visit was (sorry for sad predictability) the London version of Manet's *Execution*. Though I have spent so many hours looking at that image in the studio, I was still surprised by seeing it in the flesh again: the way the painting works at its own scale (I have almost become habituated to the image at the scale at which I am drawing it); its fragmentation (which registers more viscerally in the object itself); the effect of its missing parts (i.e., we only see the hand of the figure that is the execution's object, so there is a space left open, the absence of the figure who would be shot, which we are left to fill ourselves).

I also did some grazing on the collection. The surprise in this was Titian's *Death of Actaeon*, which made me think of the origins of your show and Pettigrew's contention on the Gwion Gwion (i.e., that the paintings are alive and renew themselves through bacteria and fungi that eat themselves, an endless process of self-devouring that is also the paintings' self-generation into the present — a process that I assume was knowingly triggered by the artists who, many thousands of years ago, first made those paintings). I am not sure if you have ever spent much time with that Titian painting, but part of what is striking is the different painterly or material treatment in different parts of the picture.

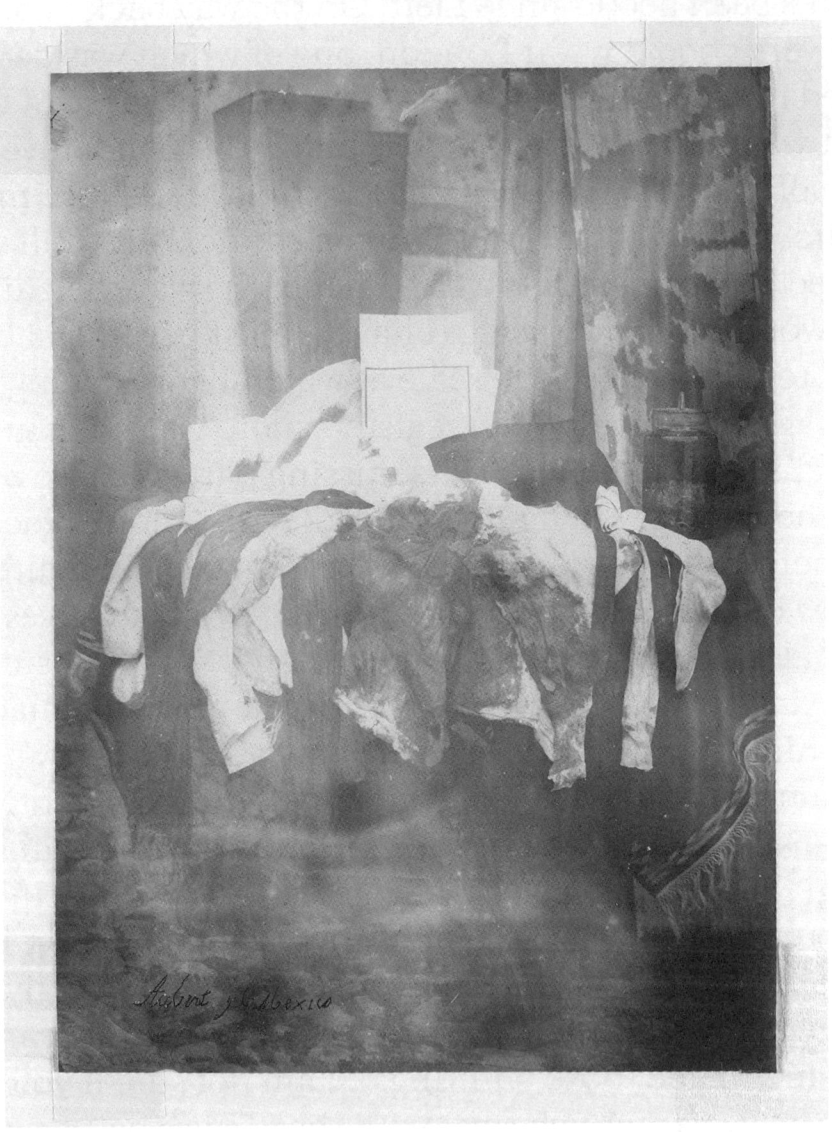
Aubert y Ca Mexico

In the section where Actaeon is turned into a stag to be devoured by his own hounds (i.e., the right-hand section of the image) the painting becomes incredibly crude, scarcely more than paint itself, so that our itinerary through the painting towards this scene of violence is both towards Actaeon (suspended at the moment before he is) consumed by his own dogs, but also towards (the suspension of) the moment when figuration is consumed by the matter of the painting. This was all the more pronounced with Manet's *Execution* in my head, where the firing of a lethal projectile is figured like one moment endlessly repeated, with that Manet coolness, a Warhol-like repetition (by which I mean, all those soldiers, almost cut-out replicas of one another, all performing that same instant, like a Muybridge that does not work or progress, with all the figures then cut out and stacked into one frame). By contrast, Titian's painting has the moment of the firing and what follows all within one frame, a series of unfolding events in one picture. The arrow is absent, but the scene races to transform itself ahead of the protagonist's act of firing to become the materiality of paint, towards another kind of devouring, where the picture devours its scene.

Enclosed is a print of that picture (weird still life with Maximilian's clothes, plus mysterious monochrome/imageless picture!) that I know you love so much, which I just received as a high-res file from MoMA. By the time you get this I guess we will have skyped about your visit and the details for the trip to

Lake Mungo. When we skype, I'll make sure I also mention the experience of spending the day with Courbet's *The artist's studio*, which also had my mind racing about all this.

Big hugs.
Tom

Dear 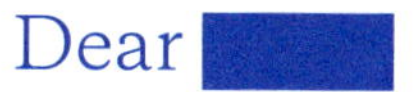

Enclosed are photocopies of all the *Novara* material I looked at while I was in Vienna. As I think I mentioned when we spoke on the phone, I spent quite a bit of time trying to locate about 50 *Novara* objects from Sydney that are now missing. (I was never able to locate these, despite visits to various departments where they might have been mistakenly stored. They seem to be lost without trace.)

I also followed a long set of leads about Bungaree, to try to find out whether Scherzer did take his skull from the Museum in Sydney during the *Novara*'s time on the Harbour. Looking into this question was pretty gross and upsetting (the grave-robbing of the ancestors of people who are dear friends). Though I sometimes wondered if I was becoming like Scherzer himself, digging around amidst all these skeletal remains, I figured it was a chance to find out if Bungaree's skull really was taken to Vienna, a chance to collect information that might inform an effort towards repatriation. The curator in the Anthropology Department at the Natural History Museum said that two skulls, listed as having been brought back from Sydney by the *Novara*, apparently ended up in the Anatomy Department collection of the Medicine School of Vienna University, now the Medical University Vienna (one of these could perhaps be Bungaree's skull, if your hunch is right). From there they could have ended up in the Pathology and

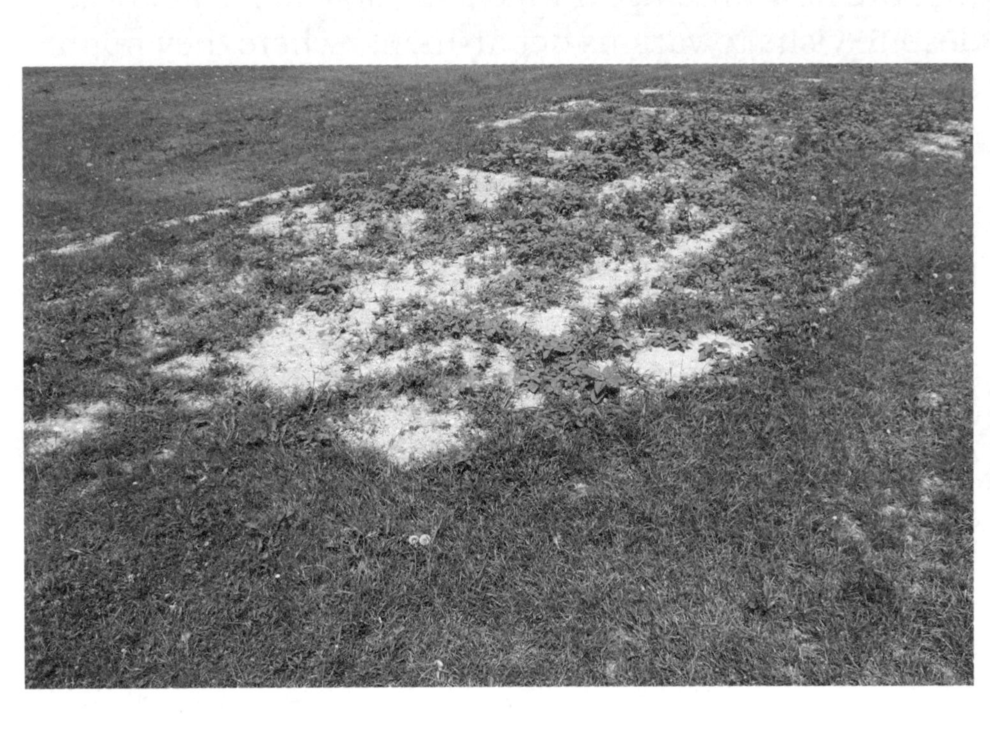

Anatomy Museum, a truly strange museum now housed in the *Narrenturm* ('Fool's Tower', translated literally), Europe's first mental asylum. When I visited, there was no evidence of the skulls being there, though I did see some of the most remarkable objects of my stay in Vienna: the lungs of two nineteenth-century coal miners preserved and displayed in jars, the incredibly ornate patterning of the lungs marked out by the black dust that fills and ultimately destroys their respiratory systems. At the Medical University, I was told that the skulls may have been in their Anatomy Department collection, but that a significant part of this collection was destroyed by a huge fire caused by an Allied bomb in the last days of the Second World War. More recently, it came to light that part of the Anatomy Department's collection came from Jewish prisoners executed by the Nazis, in some cases with the collusion of the Anatomy Department itself. These remains were recently buried in the 'Anatomy Department Graveyard' in the Vienna Central Cemetery. If Scherzer did take Bungaree's skull in 1858, it is possible it was buried in this area of the Cemetery, alongside the remains of those Jewish men, women and children. I visited the Cemetery at the very end of my stay (also to visit the grave of Joseph Selleny, the artist from the *Novara* I think I mentioned I have been reading about). The photograph (also enclosed) shows this area of the Cemetery, the part dedicated to the 'Anatomy Department Graveyard', the expanse of open ground where my efforts to trace Bungaree end.

Standing in front of the bareness of that place — with no text or marker or sculpted form in view — I did find myself remembering all those paintings and lithographs and watercolours of Bungaree, all those versions of his image, standing overlooking Sydney Harbour.

I am sorry that my enquiries did not yield anything more definitive, that I did not manage to locate any visible trace of all this.

I hope to see you when I am up in Sydney next month.

Warmest regards,
Tom

Hi ██████

A short letter to say thanks for the studio visit. I enjoyed what you said about that drawing, and that desire to withdraw from showing. I've been reading up about solarisation since we spoke.

And thanks for photographing the current state of the trial wall drawing. I tend to think the photographs of small fragments of the wall drawing are better than the attempt to capture the wall in its totality, an attempt the drawing does not really allow.

I also like the suggestion you made about Ian Burn's Xerox works, the echo between his accumulations of photocopy artefact and the aggregation of all those airborne particles of charcoal on my studio wall.

As promised, enclosed is the Lanzmann autobiography. The last two chapters on *Shoah* are the book's most compelling parts, though there is also a curious narrative in there about a kind of (unrealised) love affair in North Korea, an experience in love that he wanted to make a film about, but that somehow resisted becoming images.

Just following up that conversation about artists' last works, I meant to say that as part of that same project I have been looking at a Viennese artist, Joseph Selleny, who spent some time in Sydney in late 1858 (sponsored by Maximilian, on the *Novara*). He was a protégé of Maximilian. As far as I can tell, he was very close to him personally, and went mad not long after Maximilian's execution (eventually dying in an asylum just outside Vienna in 1875). When I was in Vienna last year I sought out his last painting, which I ultimately saw in the underground store of the Wien Museum. It is the strangest thing: a huge phantasmagoric, hyper-kitsch, ornate cornucopia landscape, or *Urwald* ('Primeval forest'), as the title of the painting states. The weird thing is that this last finished painting by Selleny, created immediately after Maximilian's execution in 1867, made on the cusp of his madness, is an image from his time in Sydney. I don't know why an image from Sydney is in his mind at that point, why he makes that particular painting upon Maximilian's execution, something from a decade earlier in his life. It's a truly strange last work, both a response to his patron's death, and, in the narrative of his own life, the anticipation of his own. The charge of the work is in its extraordinary detail, something that marks every moment of the painting, like thousands of microscopic views on to the world sutured together into a hallucination. I can't help wondering what it is that is actually being pictured here, beyond what the painting literally shows, behind its 'screen'. In a strange way, that wall drawing you photographed in my studio, which began as a tentative effort to make a map of the world turned into a series of points, has become an attempt to make the outlines of that extraordinarily, ornately detailed *Urwald*: an array of points that would delineate that remembered image from Sydney which for some reason surfaces as Selleny's last picture, the last image he makes before the madness that follows Maximilian's execution engulfs him. I'm not sure if that's what my wall drawing finally pictures, what it is that is being drawn here.

See you at the studio next week.

Cheers,
Tom

Selected bibliography

Akademie der Wissenschafter (ed.), *Reise der österreichischen Fregatte Novara um die Erde in den Jahren 1857, 1858, 1859 unter den Befehlen des Commodore B. von Wüllerstorf-Urbair. Zoologischer Theil. 1. Band (Wirbelthiere)* (Vienna: Akademie der Wissenschafter, 1869).

——, *Reise der österreichischen Fregatte Novara um die Erde in den Jahren 1857, 1858, 1859 unter den Befehlen des Commodore B. von Wüllerstorf-Urbair. Zoologischer Theil. 2. Band (Wirbelthiere)* (Vienna: Akademie der Wissenschafter, 1868).

——, *Reise der österreichischen Fregatte Novara um die Erde in den Jahren 1857, 1858, 1859 unter den Befehlen des Commodore B. von Wüllerstorf-Urbair. Zoologischer Theil. 2. Bände (Wirbelthiere)* (Vienna: Akademie der Wissenschafter, 1864 and 1866).

Attenbrow, Val, *Sydney's Aboriginal Past: Investigating the Archaeological and Historical Records* (Sydney: University of New South Wales Press, 2002).

Badiou, Alain, with Nicolas Truong, *In Praise of Love* (London: Serpent's Tail, 2012).

Bambach, Carmen C., *Drawing and Painting in the Italian Renaissance Workshop. Theory and Practice, 1300-1600* (Cambridge: Cambridge University Press, 1999).

Beutler, Gigi, *The Imperial Vaults of the PP Capuchins in Vienna* (Vienna: Beutler-Heldenstein Publications, 2007).

Clark, C. M. H., *A History of Australia*, vol. 1 (Melbourne: Melbourne University Press, 1974).

Clendinnen, Inga, *Dancing with Strangers* (Melbourne: Text Publishing, 2005).

Collins, David, *An Account of the English Colony in New South Wales*, 2 vols, facs. ed. (Adelaide: Libraries Board of South Australia, 1971; first published London: T. Cadell and W. Davies, 1798).

Dawes, Lieutenant William, *Vocabulary of the language of N. S. Wales, in the neighbourhood of Sydney (Native and English)*, [Notebooks], ML 41645A and 41645B, FM4/3431.

Der Freie Weite Horizont. Die Weltumseglung der Novara und Maximilians Mexikanerischer Traum, exh. cat. (Tirol: Castel Tirolo/Schloss Tirol, 2004).

Elderfield, John, *Manet and the Execution of Maximilian*, exh. cat. (New York: Museum of Modern Art, 2006).

Fath, Manfred and Stefan Germer (eds.), *Edouard Manet: Augenblicke der Gesichte*, exh. cat. (Mannheim: Städtischen Kunsthalle Mannheim, Munich: Prestel-Verlag, 1992).

Flannery, Tim (ed.), *The Birth of Sydney* (Melbourne: Text Publishing, 1999).

——, *Terra Australis. Matthew Flinders' Great Adventures in the Circumnavigation of Australia* (Melbourne: Text Publishing, 2000; first published as *A voyage to Terra Australis*, 1814).

Fletcher, J. E., 'Karl Scherzer and the Visit of the Novara to Sydney, 1858', *Journal of the Royal Australian Historical Society*, 71(3), December 1985, pp. 189-206.

——, 'The Novara in Sydney, November-December 1858: on unlocking a time-warp', in W. Boyd Rayward (ed.), *Australian Library History in Context: Papers for the Third Forum on Australian Library History, University of New South Wales, 17 and 18 July 1987* (Sydney: School of Librarianship, University of New South Wales, 1988), pp. 7-25.

——, 'Joseph Selleny', in J. Kerr (ed), *The Dictionary of Australian Artists. Painters, Sketchers, Photographers and Engravers to 1870* (Melbourne: Oxford University Press, 1992), pp. 712-4.

Frauenfeld, Georg von, *Tagebücher 1-9 (Novara-Tagebücher 1-5)* (Vienna: Naturhistorisches Museum in Wien, 2001), Sammlung Frauenfeld Inv.-Nr.: 166.01-166.09.

——, *Die naturhistorischen und ethnographsichen Sammlungen erworben während der Weltfahrt SR. K. k. apost. Majestät Kriegsfregatte >Novara< unter Commando des Commodore Freiherren Bernhard von Wüllerstorf-Urbair* (Vienna: Naturhistorisches Museum in Wien, 1863).

Goodhall, Heather, *Invasion to Embassy: Land and Aboriginal Politics in New South Wales, 1770-1972* (Sydney: Allen & Unwin, 1996).

Grenville, Kate, *The Secret River* (Melbourne: Text Publishing, 2005).

Hochstetter, Ferdinand von, *Gessamelte Reise-Berichte von der Erdumsegelung der Fregatte >Novara< 1857–1859* (Vienna: Akademie der Wissenschafter, 1885).

Karskens, Grace, *The Colony: A History of Early Sydney* (Sydney: Allen & Unwin, 2009).

Lanzmann, Claude, *The Patagonian Hare*, translated by Frank Wynne (London: Atlantic Books, 2012).

Müller, Friedrich, *Reise der österreichischen Fregatte Novara um die Erde in den Jahren 1857, 1858, 1859 unter den Befehlen des Commodore B. von Wüllerstorf-Urbair. Anthropologischer Theil, Dritte Abteilung: Ethnographie auf Grund des von Dr. Karl Scherzer gesammelten Materials* (Vienna: Akademie der Wissenschafter, 1864).

——, *Reise der österreichischen Fregatte Novara um die Erde in den Jahren 1857, 1858, 1859 unter den Befehlen des Commodore B. von Wüllerstorf-Urbair. Linguistischer Theil* (Vienna: Akademie der Wissenschafter, 1867).

——, *Reise der österreichischen Fregatte Novara um die Erde in den Jahren 1857, 1858, 1859 unter den Befehlen des Commodore B. von Wüllerstorf-Urbair. Anthropologischer Theil (3. Abteilung: Ethnographie)* (Vienna: Akademie der Wissenschafter, 1868).

Orchard, Ken, Michael Organ and John Walsh, *Illawarra: The Garden of New South Wales*, exh. cat. (Wollongong: Wollongong City Gallery, 1994).

Organ, Michael, *The Austrian Frigate SMS Novara*, website: http://www.uow.edu.au/~morgan/novara.htm (Wollongong: University of Wollongong, 2010).

Organ, Michael, J. E. Fletcher and G. Vladar, 'Joseph Selleny: An Austrian Artist in New South Wales, November–December 1858', published at www.uow.edu.au/~morgan/novara5.htm (Wollongong: University of Wollongong, 2011).

Patzak, Beatrix, *Faszination und Ekel: Das Pathologisch-anatomische Bundemuseum im Wiener Narrenturm* (Graz: Verlag F. Sammler, 2009).

Pettigrew, Jack, Chloe Callistemon, Astrid Weiler, Anna Gorbushina, Wolfgang Krumbein and Reto Weiler, 'Living pigments in Australian Bradshaw rock art', *Antiquity*, Volume 084, Issue 326, December 2010, online at http://antiquity.ac.uk/projgall/pettigrew326/

Philip, Arthur, *The Voyage of Arthur Philip to Botany Bay* (London: J. Stockdale, 1789; facs. ed. Sydney: Hutchinson, 1982).

Popelka, Liselotte and Friedrich Hausmann, *Joseph Selleny und seine Aquarelle von der Weltreise der Novara, 1857–1859* (Graz: H. Böhlaus Nachf., 1963).

Reynolds, Henry, *The Other Side of the Frontier: Aboriginal Resistance to the European Invasion of Australia* (Melbourne: Penguin, 1983).

——, *The Whispering in Our Hearts* (Sydney: Allen & Unwin, 1998).

——, *The Question of Genocide in Australia's History: An Indelible Stain?* (Melbourne: Viking, 2001).

Riedl-Dorn, Christa, *Blumen eines Kaisers. Maximilian von Mexiko und seine Brasilienreise 1859–1860* (Vienna: Österreichisches Landesmuseum, 1992).

Scherzer, Karl von, *Reise der österreichischen Fregatte Novara um die Erde in den Jahren 1857, 1858, 1859 unter den Befehlen des Commodore B. von Wüllerstorf-Urbair. Statistisch-Commercieller Theil, zwei Bände* (Vienna: Hof- und Staatsdruckerei, 1864).

——, *Reise der österreichischen Fregatte Novara um die Erde in den Jahren 1857, 1858, 1859 unter den Befehlen des Commodore B. von Wüllerstorf-Urbair. Beschreibender Theil, drei Bände* (Vienna: Hof- und Staatsdruckerei, 1864–6).

——, *Reise der österreichischen Fregatte Novara um die Erde in den Jahren 1857, 1858, 1859 unter den Befehlen des Commodore B. von Wüllerstorf-Urbair. Anthropolischer Theil. Zweite Abthlung. Körpermessungen, an Individuen verschiedener Menschenracen vorgenommen durch Dr K. Scherzer und Dr E. Schwartz, bearbeitet von Dr A. Weisbach* (Vienna: Hof- und Staatsdruckerei, 1867).

——, *Narrative of the Circumnavigation of the Globe by the Austrian Frigate Novara (Commodore B. Von Wullerstorf-Urbair), Undertaken by Order of the Imperial Government in the Years 1857, 1858, & 1859, Under the Immediate Auspices of His I. and R. Highness the Archduke Ferdinand Maximilian, Commander-In-Chief of the Austrian Navy* (London: Saunders, Otley & Co., 1861–3).

——, ‘Über Körpermessungen als behelf zur Diagnostik Menschenraçen’, *Mittheilungen der k. k. Geographischen Gesellschaft*, Wien, III, 1859, pp. 11–31.

Scott, A.W., *Australian Lepidoptera and their Transformations*, illustrated by Harriett and Helena Scott and Joseph Selleny (London: J. van Voorst, 1864).

Seipel, Wilfried (ed.), *Die Entdeckung der Welt. Die Welt der Entdeckung. Österreichische Forscher, Sammler, Abenteur*, exh. cat. (Vienna: Kunsthistorischen Museum, 2002).

Smith, Keith Vincent, *King Bungaree: A Sydney Aborigine meets the great South Pacific explorers, 1799–1830* (Kenthurst, NSW: Kangaroo Press, 1992).

——, *Bennelong: The Coming in of the Eora: Sydney Cove 1788–1792* (East Roseville: Kangaroo Press; London: Viacom, 2001).

——, *Eora: Mapping Aboriginal Sydney 1770–1850*, exh. cat. (Sydney: State Library of New South Wales, 2006).

——, *Mari Nawi: Aboriginal Odysseys*, exh. cat. (Sydney: State Library of New South Wales, 2010).

Tench, Watkin, *A Narrative of the Expedition to Botany Bay and A Complete Account of the Settlement at Port Jackson*, published as *Sydney's First Four Years*, edited by L. F. Fitzhardinge (Sydney: Library of Australian History, 1979; first published 1789 and 1793).

Wilson-Bareau, Juliet, *Manet: The Execution of Maximillian. Painting, Politics and Censorship* (London, Princeton: National Gallery Publications, in association with Princeton University Press, 1992).

Index to Images

p 0 Saskia Doherty, *Untitled photograph.* 2013. Digital photograph.

4 Tom Nicholson, *Photograph of NSW boomerang and gloves, Museum für Völkerkunde, Vienna.* 2012. Digital photograph.

8 Francois Aubert, *Maximillian's shirt.* June 1867. Albumen silver print, 22 × 16.2 cm, The Getty Research Institute, Los Angeles (96.R.141).

12 Detail of Joseph Selleny, *Australischer Urwald.* 1867. Oil on canvas, 118 × 157 cm, Wien Museum, Inv-Nr 27321. Photograph: Tom Nicholson.

14 Christian Capurro, *Detail of Tom Nicholson's studio wall,* 2014. Digital photograph.

18 Tom Nicholson, *Pouncing photograph (Cartoons for Joseph Selleny).* 2014. Type C Photograph, 130 × 87 cm. Photography: Christian Capurro.

24 Francois Aubert, *Untitled (Bloody clothes from the execution of Emperor Maximilian).* 1867. Albumen silver print, 21.9 × 16.2 cm. Museum of Modern Art (MoMA), New York. Purchase. Acc. n.: SC1993.68. © 2014. Digital image, The Museum of Modern Art, New York/Scala, Florence

28 Tom Nicholson, *Photograph of 'Anatomy Department Graveyard' in the Vienna Central Cemetery.* 2012. Digital photograph.

Acknowledgements

I began to work on *Cartoons for Joseph Selleny* in early 2012 in the lead up to a Lenikus Collection residency in Vienna. The project began with a conversation with the Kamilaroi/Wiradjuri artist Jonathan Jones, who in turn was instrumental in initiating a conversation with Gorawarl/Jerrawongarla elder Auntie Julie Freeman. These two conversations remained central to the project during its long gestation and realisation, and I am grateful for the generosity, knowledge and good company of both Jonathan and Aunty Julie, from whom I learnt many things, within the scope of the project and beyond. At different times, these conversations also came to include Clive Freeman, Markeeta Freeman, Genevieve O'Callaghan and Clare Land, and I am grateful to their generosity to the project, and their knowledge.

Jasper Sharp and Francesco Stocchi kindly facilitated my Lenikus Collection residency in Vienna in June 2012, which was also supported by Angela Akbari. During this residency in Vienna my research on the *Novara* and the material gathered during her time in Sydney was assisted by many curators in different institutions: Dr Garbriele Weiss at the Museum für Völkerkunde (who was enormously generous in her engagement, in the knowledge she shared, and in establishing contacts for me in other institutions); Dr Robert Pils, Dr Karin Wiltschke-Schrotta, and Dr Verena Stagl at the Naturhistorisches Musuem in Vienna; Dr Ralph Gleis at the Wien Museum; Dr Michael Pretterklieber, Dr Ruth Koblizek, and Dr Sonia Horn at the Medical University Wien; Beatrix Patzak at the Pathology and Anatomy Museum Vienna Narreturm; Elsy Lahner and Ingrid Kastel at the Albertina.

During my stay in Vienna I met on several occasions with Helge Selleny, a descendant of Joseph Selleny, who was warm and wholehearted in his engagement with the project, including giving me innumerable valuable resources, and hosting me at his house outside Vienna to see a number of Selleny's works held in his family's collection. I thank him and his family.

At the very beginning of the project, in Australia, I could not have begun to think about the *Novara* without the extraordinary website dedicated to the *Novara* created by Michael Organ, who in turn became a generous interlocutor and facilitated my visit to the Wollongong City Gallery's store to look at Selleny's work.

Similarly, the knowledge of Keith Vincent Smith, his published work on the early history of Sydney and on Bungaree, were central parts of the project's development, as was his own personal generosity towards me and the project.

My research in Vienna was supported by a Faculty Grant from Monash Art Design and Architecture (MADA), which also supported this artist's book with a Publication Grant. During the last stages of the project I was able to focus on its finalisation through a Faculty Fellowship that relieved me of undergraduate teaching obligations. In this financial support, and in the Faculty's support of my work in a more general sense, I am indebted to many of my colleagues, especially Ruth Bain, Kathie Barwick, Dr Stephen Garrett, Professor Shane Murray, Professor Callum Morton, Sarah Oliver and Dr Kit Wise.

Thanks to the Getty Institute, MoMA and Scala for their assistance with including images from their collections in this artist's book.

The latter stages of the project could not have been realised with the intensity it required without the Creative Fellowship that was awarded to me in late 2013 by the Myer Foundation, for which I am very grateful.

Saskia Doherty's work as a studio assistant, particularly in contributing to the under-drawing of the cartoons and in the realisation of a large-scale trial wall drawing, was invaluable, as was the intelligence and depth of her engagement with all dimensions of the project. Towards the end, the project also benefitted from the drawings skills and energy of Chris Fairlie, in preparing the under-drawing of the cartoons.

It is always a pleasure to work with Brad Haylock, who designed this book, as well as the book from 2010 that is its template, *Drawings and correspondence*.

The editing skills of Roger Averill were important in refining the nine letters that make up this book.

Christian Capurro's photography—as well as his ever-critical, ever-generous words in the studio—were important to the project throughout its life.

I thank Josh Milani for his friendship, his support, in its many forms, and the sense of belief in art and artists that characterises this support.

Though *Cartoons for Joseph Selleny* precedes our conversation about *Allegory of the Cave Painting*, the project has been nourished in significant ways by Mihnea Mircan and his thinking about this exhibition. I am grateful for his intelligence, his wit, and the generosity of his friendship. Caroline van Eccelpoel and the staff at Extra City Kunsthal Antwerp have been very supportive of the project, its resourcing and its realisation. My participation in this exhibition in Antwerp was supported by a grant from the Visual Art Travel Fund of the Australia Council for the Arts.

I thank the staff at the Art Gallery of New South Wales (AGNSW). My conversation about this project included from the outset Natasha Bullock, who has been very supportive of me and the project during its long development. Cara Pinchbeck, Emily McDaniel, Diarne Wiercinski, Macushla Robinson, Nik Rieth, Thomas Cole and Joel Mu were among many staff at the AGNSW without whom the project could not have been realised.

Thanks to my family for their support during the several demanding phases of this work: Clare Land, my children Luci, Jean and Joseph, Shelley Marshall, my parents Mary and Peter Nicholson.

I acknowledge the Wurundjeri of the Kulin Nation as the original owners of the land on which I live and work. This includes an acknowledgement that the moral and legal consequences of invasion remain unresolved.

—Tom Nicholson

Cartoons for Joseph Selleny (2012–14)
Tom Nicholson

First edition 2014
ISBN: 978-1-922099-10-5

Published by Surpllus Pty Ltd
Melbourne, Australia
www.surpllus.com

Editor: Roger Averill
Design: Brad Haylock

Typeset in Galaxie Copernicus and Akzidenz Grotesk
Printed by Drukkerij Sintjoris, Belgium

This artist's book is part of the project *Cartoons for Joseph Selleny*, created for a solo exhibition of the same title, curated by Natasha Bullock, at the Art Gallery of New South Wales, Sydney, and for the exhibition *Allegory of the Cave Painting*, curated by Mihnea Mircan, at Extra City Kunsthal, Antwerp, both in 2014.

Tom Nicholson is an artist who lives and works in Melbourne. He is represented by Milani Gallery, and is a Lecturer at Monash Art Design and Architecture, Monash University.
www.tomn.net
www.milanigallery.com.au
www.artdes.monash.edu.au

Brad Haylock is Associate Professor of Design in the School of Media and Communication at RMIT University.
www.bradhaylock.com
www.rmit.edu.au/mediacommunication

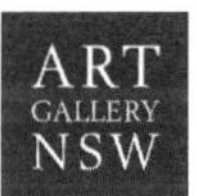

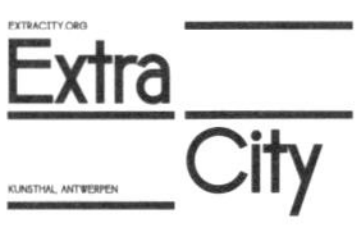

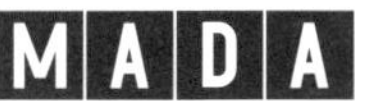

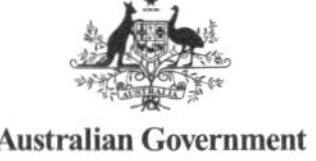

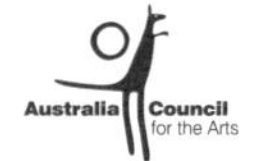

SURPLLUS #17